How to be Brilliant at
MAKING
BOOKS

Brilliant Publications

We hope you and your class will enjoy using this book. Other books in the series include:

How to be Brilliant at Writing Stories   1 897675 00 3
How to be Brilliant at Writing Poetry   1 897675 01 1
How to be Brilliant at Grammar   1 897675 02 X

If you would like further information on these or other titles published by Brilliant Publications, write to the address given below.

Published by Brilliant Publications,
PO Box 143, Leamington Spa CV31 1EB

Written by Irene Yates
Illustrated by Kate Ford
Cover photograph by Martyn Chillmaid

Printed in Great Britain by the Warwick
Printing Company Ltd

© Irene Yates 1993
ISBN 1 897675 03 8

First published in 1993
10 9 8 7 6 5 4 3 2 1

Contents

Introduction 4
Links to the National Curriculum 5

Presentation
Good titles 6
Super writing 7
Be a graphic designer 8
Eye-catching titles 9
Get into technology 10
Be an illustrator 11
Illuminated letters 12
Edge of the page 13
Keeping the pages together 14
Putting the pages together 15
Choosing chapters 16
Creating an index 17
Preliminary pages 18
Deadline! 19

Techniques
Speaking mouth pop-ups 20
Triangle pop-ups 21
Two-sided pop-ups 22
Surprise pop-ups 23
Concertinas 24
What shape? 25
Flick-through books 26

Books with windows 27
Flap books 28
Pocket books 29
Books on the wall 30
Mini-books 31

Ideas for books
Who will read it? 32
Scrap-books 33
Collection books 34
Albums 35
Diaries and journals 36
Making a group book 37
Class books 38
Swap-with-a-friend books 39
Poetry anthologies 40
Picture story-books 41
Talking books 42
Books for information 43
Books of retold stories 44
Make an official family history book 45
How to... books 46

Check-list of things to think about when making books 47

Glossary 48

Introduction

How to be Brilliant at Making Books contains 42 photocopiable ideas for use with 7-11 year olds. The book provides a flexible, but structured, resource for encouraging children to write and to value their writing.

The sheets are self-explanatory and ready to use; the only extra resources needed are a pen or pencil and sometimes drawing materials and extra paper. Use of the computer is a bonus and a word-processing program, used whenever possible, should facilitate drafting and redrafting.

The making of books provides motivation and a purpose for writing. Children are led into a greater appreciation and awareness of audience and begin to develop their own critical evaluation skills. The photocopiable sheets encourage a wide range of skills allowing the children to:
• compose
• create
• publish
• respond to print.

The technological side of book production involves lots of problem-solving and engages the children in gathering information, prioritizing, negotiating, decision-making and evaluating.

A crucial factor in writing and making books is sharing them with an audience. Children benefit enormously from the feedback they receive when their writing and books have been shared and valued. The ideas in this book need not be restricted to your language lessons and can be used to enhance all areas of the curriculum.

Give your pupils plenty of flexibility and freedom to make the books how they want them. They will have their own ideas and will gain from their ownership.

The majority of activities are open-ended. Answers are given below for the two which are not:

Page 6
The well-known book is *Winnie the Pooh*.

Page 18
Title pages always show the title and sometimes also the author and/or the publisher.

The copyright symbol always has the year the book was published and the copyright holder (who is usually either the author or the publisher).

Acknowledgements are most commonly given for photo credits, text credits and thanks.

All books printed in the UK will state who the printer is, but this is not a requirement abroad.

Each publisher has its own ISBN prefix. For example, 1 897675 is the prefix for Brilliant Publications. Larger publishers usually have shorter prefixes.

Links to the National Curriculum

The following Key Stage 2 Programmes of Study for English are covered in this book (taken from the Department for Education's April 1993 document):

Pupils should:
*   continue to write for the varied purposes identified at Key Stage 1, understanding that writing is essential to thinking and learning and enjoyable in itself. They should be taught to use writing as a means of organizing and communicating ideas and that it will require confident use of a wider range of vocabulary choice, grammatical structures and punctuation;

*   be taught to develop their writing beyond a first draft, learning to:
    *   **plan:** note and develop initial ideas;
    *   **draft:** ideas from the plan are developed into structured written text;
    *   **revise:** the draft is altered to make meaning clear *(eg remove ambiguity, vagueness)*; consider choices of vocabulary;
    *   **proof-read:** checking for spelling and punctuation errors, omissions or repetitions;
    *   **present** a neat, correct and clear final copy;

*   be taught to consider the effectiveness of their writing and how it can be improved;

*   be provided with an extended range of audiences for writing, including the teacher, the class, younger and older children, adults in the school or community and imagined audiences;

*   be taught to use the characteristics of different kinds of writing. The forms in which they write should include: poetry; stories; letters; notes; diaries; reports; instructions; dialogue and drama scripts; explanations;

*   be taught to use features of layout, *eg headings, sub-headings* to clarify presentation;

*   write clearly for different audiences, maintaining the reader's interest;

*   convey meaning clearly, drafting work to refine ideas, eliminate ambiguities or extend a narrative or argument. They should be taught to edit their work and present it effectively.

Good titles

The title may be the first thing you read when you pick up a book, but it's not always the first thing you need to think about when writing. Sometimes it's better to choose a title after the book is written.

A good title makes people curious about your book.

Think of a story you have written recently. With a friend, brainstorm ideas for your title using the following methods. Try to find two ideas for each method:

Alliteration (words beginning with the same sound)

_____

_____

Rhyme

_____

_____

A phrase from the book

_____

_____

Discuss which is best.

Guess the book!

Here are alternative titles for a well-known book. Guess what the real title is.

- Bear of no Brain

- Funny Runny Honey!

- Rum-tum-tiddle-um-tum

My guess _____

Think up your own alternative title for this well-known book:

Teacher: see page 4 for answer.

EXTRA!
Look at 10 books in the library or your classroom. Choose which titles you like best.
Try to decide why you like them. Think up 10 new titles for the books.
Ask a friend to guess which are the real titles and which are yours.

Super writing

You can make your books look really good by choosing different styles of lettering for your titles and headings.

Here are some ideas:

ABCDEFGHIJKLMNOPQRSTUVWXYZ

abcdefghijklmnopqrstuvwxyz

ABCDEFGHIJKLMNOPQRSTUVWXYZ

ABCDEFGHIJKLMNOPQRSTUVWXYZ abcdefghijklmn opqrstuvwxyz

Practise these lettering styles here:

EXTRA!
Use the back of this sheet to create five more lettering styles of your own.

How to be Brilliant at Making Books

Be a graphic designer

Graphic designers are the people who design books. They plan how each page will look before they begin to put a book together. These plans are called 'page layouts' and they should tell you exactly where everything will go.

The way you design your page makes a lot of difference to how the finished book will look. For example, suppose you have lots of text and two pictures. Discuss with a friend which of these four page layouts you prefer. Why?

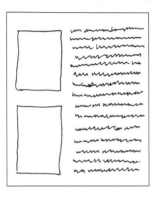   

Now, suppose you have some text and three pictures. Be a graphic designer and design five different page layouts.

EXTRA!
Use a reference book from your classroom or library and draw page layouts of three different pages as a graphic designer might have done them. How could you change them? Cut and paste your page layouts to see how different they would look.

Eye-catching titles

Usually titles are written across the top of the page, but there's nothing to say they have to be.

Here are four ways you might design your title page to catch the reader's eye.

Make up titles for six stories you have written or would like to write.
Design a title page for each here:

EXTRA!
With a friend, look for 10 different ways titles are shown on the covers of published books. Choose which you like best and try to work out why you like them.

How to be Brilliant at Making Books

Get into technology

A word-processing program on the computer can really help you with writing and designing your book.

You can draft, revise and edit

A computer is much more than a typewriter

You can move bits of text around

You can do page layouts

You can use different fonts

Find out what your machine and your program will do by:

You can change things all the time – words, spellings, spaces...

- talking to someone who knows

- experimenting

- working with a friend

- reading the instructions

- being confident enough to have a go

With a friend, write an article on 'How to use the computer for writing books'. Make sure you point out all its advantages. Can you think of any disadvantages?

Brainstorm some ideas for your article here:

You can use the back of the sheet if you run out of space.

EXTRA!
Use the computer to draft and edit all your books. When you work as a group,
take turns to be on the keyboard.

Be an illustrator

Pictures have purpose. They make the story or text more interesting to the reader. So pictures (or artwork, as editors call it) should always enhance (make better) the writing. Pictures can show what's happening and can add to the words. They have to be well thought out and that is often the editor's job.

Here are two different ideas for books, both on the same theme. Draw pictures to illustrate the covers. Give each book a catchy, but suitable, title.

This book is a story about a cat's adventures in a thunderstorm.

This book is a reference book about cats, written to tell the readers how to look after their pet.

EXTRA!
Act as an editor. Make up an outline for a book and swap with a friend.
Suggest how your friend's book should be illustrated. Then write and illustrate the books!

Illuminated letters

Before printing presses were invented, all books (every single copy!) had to be written by hand. The job belonged mostly to the monks in the abbeys and they devised a way of embellishing the first letter on each page to make it really decorative. The letters were painted (using pens made out of old goose bones) with vegetable dyes and gold leaf to make them really beautiful.

Colour in the three letters here.

Choose six letters of the alphabet to illuminate yourself. (You could start by writing your initials.)

EXTRA!
Make up a whole alphabet of illuminated letters and keep it somewhere safe so that you can cut the letters out and use them for your books.

Edge of the page

Decorative borders always make pages look well presented. You need to practise the patterns carefully first. When you can do them really well, with a steady hand, use felt tips to do them around your pages.

Start with easy patterns but try to get them perfect.

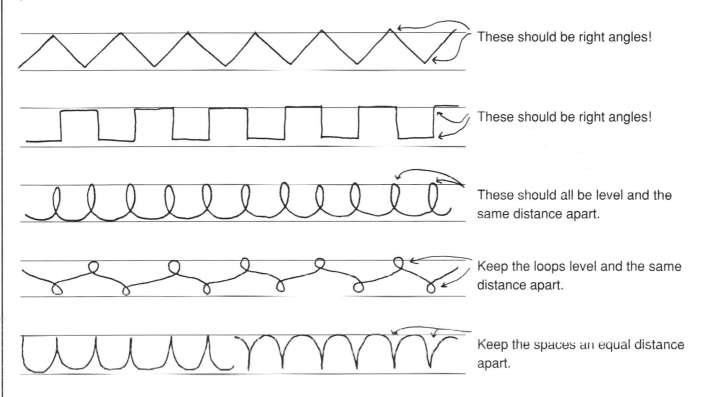

These should be right angles!

These should be right angles!

These should all be level and the same distance apart.

Keep the loops level and the same distance apart.

Keep the spaces an equal distance apart.

You can put these patterns together to form really interesting ones.

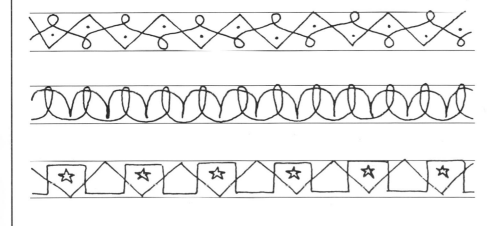

EXTRA!
The corners often get missed out or tangled up. Work out some interesting, decorative corners to use on your pages.

How to be Brilliant at Making Books

Keeping the pages together

Printers and publishers call the way they fix the pages together the 'binding'. They use machines, but you'll be doing your binding by hand. Here are some different ways you can do it:

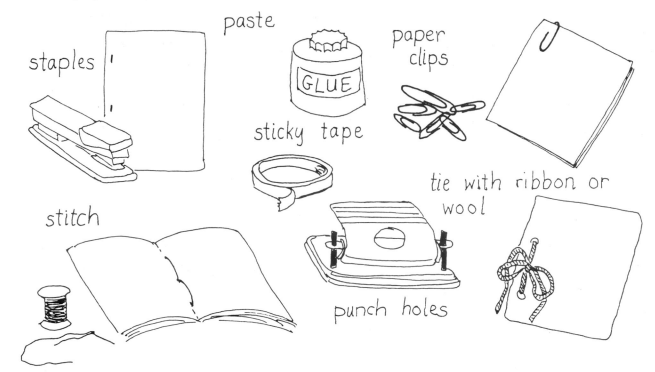

Make a list of all the advantages and disadvantages of each of the methods shown.

Practise each method and decide which is best for you and your book.

Putting the pages together

When pages are printed for a book they're not done one by one. The printer takes huge sheets of paper, which show pages in multiples of eight. The pages have to be placed very strictly otherwise they would all be in the wrong order when the book was put together.

Try this: fold a piece of paper in half and then in half again. Keep the fold at the top and number the eight pages. When you open it out, it should look like the diagram.

front

6	7
3	2

back

8	5
1	4

Take another piece of paper, fold it in half, then half again, then half again. Keep the last fold at the top; you'll have to poke your fingers in and out to number the pages. Open it out flat and see if you can fill in the missing numbers on this 16-page diagram.

front
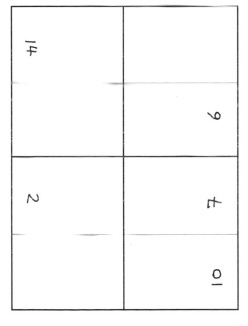

back
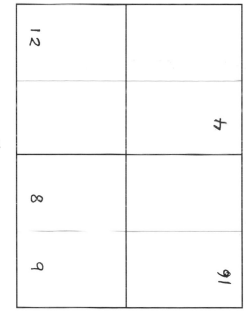

There is a rule to help you: the numbers of each pair of adjacent (side by side) pages should add up to one more than the total number of pages.

EXTRA!
Try these out. Start with the 8-page sheet. Cut where the fold is and staple the centre.
You should have a book. Then do the 16-page one. If you're really clever you
might be able to do a 32-page layout! Fill your books with your best ideas.

Choosing chapters

Lots of books, particularly reference and information books, are split into chapters. It's a very good way of organizing your work because if you do a chapter outline first you always know what's going to come next. Also, if you get stuck on one chapter you can go on to another and come back to it later. You should give each chapter a title or heading and outline what will be in it.

Use the contents pages of books to find out what they are about

For example:

Caring for your cat

Chapter 1 **Kittens.** Things to look for when buying a kitten.
Chapter 2 **Food.** What your cat needs for its diet. Water. Milk. What kind of cat food. When to feed it.
Chapter 3 **Exercise.** What cats like to play with. How to keep them in top condition.

And so on...

Choose a title for a reference book of your own. It can be about a pet, an animal, a period in history, sports, a game – make it something you're really interested in. Work out your chapter outlines here. Your book can have as many chapters as you like.

Your title:

Chapter 1

Chapter 2

Chapter 3

Chapter 4

Chapter 5

Chapter 6

Chapter 7

Chapter 8

EXTRA!
Write your book using your chapter outlines. Create a table of contents for the book. Make it look good.

How to be Brilliant at Making Books

16

Creating an index

If you've written an information or reference book, it will need an index at the back of the book. The reader uses the index to find out which pages certain things are on.

To compile an index you need your book and a piece of paper. Begin at the start of your book and note down on your paper any word that you think should be in your index, as well as the number of the page it's on.

When you've gone through the whole book, write each word and page number on a piece of card. If you get the same word more than once put it on the same piece of card.

Now put your cards into alphabetical order. Write out the index in that order clearly on a clean sheet of paper.

Make a quiz

Use a reference book. Open it up at random; write a question about a fact on that page. Do this with five more pages. Pass your quiz to a friend who *must* use the index to find the answers.

EXTRA!
Use a database on the computer to create an index.

How to be Brilliant at Making Books

Preliminary pages

Have a look at any published book and you'll see there are usually general pages at the beginning before the story or information starts. These pages are called 'preliminary pages'. Look through books and check that you can find all the things listed below. You will need to examine the preliminary pages carefully so that you can fill in the missing words.

What does 'preliminary' mean?

Look it up!

title page	The title page always shows the _____ and sometimes shows the _____.
copyright symbol	This always has the _____ the book was published.
author	Name three books by the same author: _____, _____ and _____.
acknowledgements	How many different kinds of acknowledgement can you find? List them: _____ _____
publisher's name and address	Name three publishers here: _____, _____ and _____.
printers	All books printed in _____ have the name of the printer in them, but those printed _____ may not.
ISBN	Find two or more books by the same publisher. What do you notice about the ISBNs? _____ _____

Teacher: see page 4 for answers.

Remember to allow for the preliminary pages when you're working out your pagination, that is, the number of pages needed.

EXTRA!
Get together with a friend and work as editor on each other's books to organize the preliminary pages.

How to be Brilliant at Making Books

Deadline!

Publication Day is the day you bring your book (or books) to the public and you want them to be the very best they can be. Make a check-list of everything you have to do so that you can use it to check your progress with every book you make.

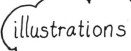

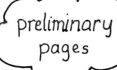

EXTRA!
Discuss your check-list with a friend to see if it contains everything.

How to be Brilliant at Making Books

Speaking mouth pop-ups

Pop-ups are really easy to do, but make your books much more interesting. Follow these instructions to make a speaking mouth pop-up.

1. You need a sheet of paper, folded in half.

2. Mark a line about 2 cm long in the centre of the side with the fold, and cut.

3. Fold the two cut edges back to form a triangle. Press the creases hard.

4. Open the page again. You will have two triangular shapes with a cut in the middle. Push the two folded edges of the first triangle through. Do this with the other triangle.

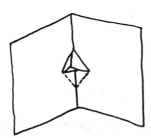

5. When you open and shut your page the triangles will look like a speaking mouth. Draw your character around it.

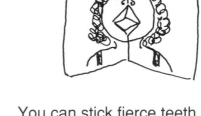

6. You can stick fierce teeth in the mouth to make it into a monster.

7. Do several pop-up pages. Before you fasten them together to make a book, glue another sheet of paper to each page to act as a backing sheet. Be careful not to get glue on the speaking mouth part!

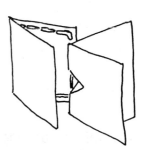

EXTRA!
Make a speaking mouth greetings card for someone.

Triangle pop-ups

Take a sheet of paper and fold it in half.

On the side with the fold, fold the top corner down to make a triangle. (Make sure you're folding the right side!) Press the crease with your fingers.

 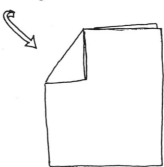

Unfold the triangle and open the sheet. Push the triangle into the middle.

On a smaller piece of paper draw a character or an object to pop-up. Cut it out and fold it vertically (keep your drawing on the outside).

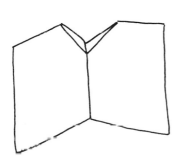  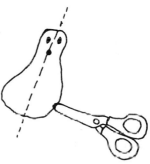

Fit the fold of the pop-up over the fold of the triangle and when you've got it absolutely straight, glue it.

Do several pop-up pages for your book, but don't forget to stick a backing sheet to each page before you bind the book together.

EXTRA!
Make a triangle pop-up greeting card for someone.

How to be Brilliant at Making Books

Two-sided pop-ups

1. Take a sheet of paper and fold it in half. Draw two lines about 2.5 cm long on the side with the fold. Cut them.

2. Fold the cut part back and press the crease with your fingers. Unfold it.

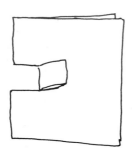

3. Open the paper up and push the folded part through to the middle.

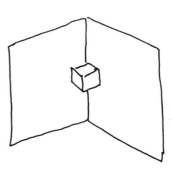

4. Draw characters and objects. Cut them out and stick them to the pop-up.

You can do several pop-up pages like this. Remember you will need to stick a backing sheet to each page before you bind them together.

Surprise pop-ups

1.   Take a sheet of paper and fold it in half. Fold down a large triangle on the folded side. Press it hard, then fold back the triangle.

2.   Draw a shaped line across the triangle about one third of the way down the sheet.

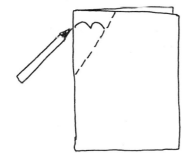

3.   Cut along the shaped line. Stop when you get to the edge of the triangle.

4.   Open the page. Pull the cut part down to make a pop-up bit. When you glue a backing sheet on to your sheet, the pop-up bit will form a pocket.

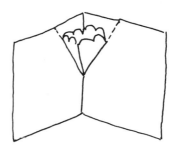

5.   Stick bits and pieces inside.

6   If you turn the sheet upside down the pop-up will form a skirt.

Practise this pop-up and develop it for yourself to make a pop-up book.

EXTRA!
Now you know the basics, develop your own ideas for making pop-ups.

Concertinas

Concertina books are good to handle and to display. You can have them going vertically or horizontally.

You need a long, thin piece of strong paper or card.

- Fold it in half first. Open it up.

- Then fold each half carefully in half. Open it up.

- Fold each quarter carefully in half.

If you don't open the paper up each time, your creases will become very uneven. Fold the creases backwards and forwards to make a concertina. Sharpen the folded edges by running a pencil or ruler along them.

Decide whether your book will be horizontal or vertical and where it will begin. Will you use both sides of the pages? If you do, be careful. Work out what happens when you turn the page over.

You can write straight on to the pages or prepare your text and illustrations on separate sheets, then cut and paste them.

Practise with scrap paper first. You can use old computer print-out paper. Cut the paper into narrow strips and glue card on to the back to make it stronger.

EXTRA!
Work with a friend to produce a concertina book of your favourite poems.
Copy them out neatly, then cut and paste them into your concertina book.

What shape?

Although most printed books are oblong in shape, yours doesn't need to be. You can make your books any shape you like!

You will have to watch your binding. If you do flower or circular shapes make sure you've chosen a way of fixing the pages together safely.

Design book shapes for:

castles   *dinosaurs*

transport   *shells*

adventure on a
tropical island

EXTRA!
Choose one of
your designs to
write, illustrate
and publish.

How to be Brilliant at Making Books

Flick-through books

Flick-through books are easy to do, but great fun. You need lots of pages, fixed together.

A flick-through book works on the same principle as a cartoon film. You draw the pictures (frames), one to each page, and when you flick the pages between your finger and thumb you see the pictures move.

Try this example for showing a flower growing. Finish the pictures then colour them in. Cut them out and staple the pages in order. Flick through them to see the story.

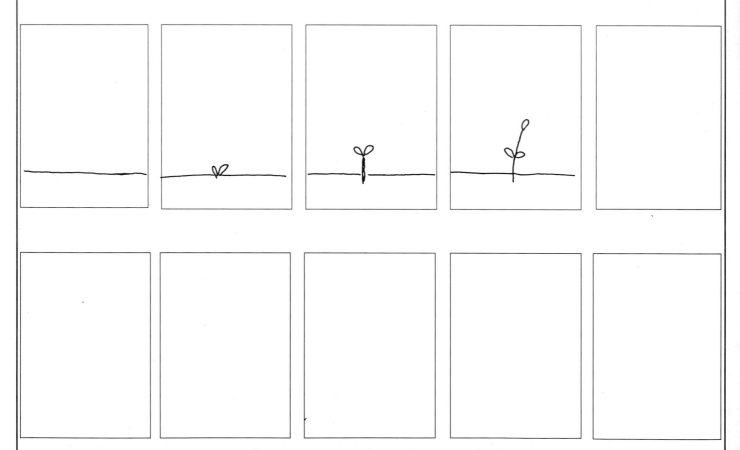

> **EXTRA!**
> Make a flick-through book of a rocket taking off and landing on the moon.
> Share it with a friend.

Books with windows

Before you make a window book, do this to practise:

You will need four pieces of paper or card. Lay them on top of one another.

Draw a picture on the first sheet. Choose something interesting in the picture and cut round it to make a small window.

On the second sheet, through the space, draw in the missing bit of the picture. Turn the first sheet over. Now draw a different picture on the second sheet around the bit you've already drawn.

Choose something interesting in the second picture and cut out a window.

On the third sheet, draw the bit that's missing through the window.

Turn that sheet over and finish the drawing. Do the same with the fourth sheet.

When you've finished, cut it out and fix the pages together to see how the windows work. Use it as a model to make your own book.

EXTRA!
Examine a copy of *The Very Hungry Caterpillar*, by Eric Carle to see how its windows work.

Flap books

Books are always more interesting if they have bits that open and close. A flap book can be fun because it can tell one story in the text and on top of the flaps, and another story underneath the flaps.

Flaps can be made to open upwards, downwards, or sideways.

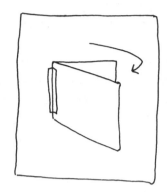

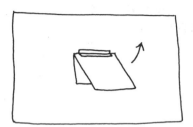

They can be stuck on very easily with sticky tape. Stick the tape to both sides of the flap to make it stronger. You'll need to cut the tape exactly the length of the flap, otherwise the flap won't open properly.

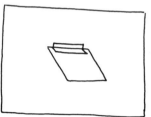

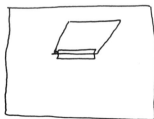

Try this idea for a flap book

Make a picture story-book about Growler the Dog. Make the words and the top flap pictures show Growler to be a very fierce animal, but make the words and the pictures underneath the flaps show him to be a softie.

Work out your words and pictures here.

EXTRA!
When you've sorted out the whole story, make the book.

Run out of space? Use the back of the sheet!

Pocket books

Young children love to have books with bits that move about.

Choose a story with a strong main character. You could use a story you have made up or you could use a story you've read that you'd like to retell.

Make up your book and put the text, illustrations and decorations in. You will need a heavy card cover and an extra piece of card to tape on to the front to make a pocket.

Tape the sides and the bottom. Leave the top open so that it makes a pocket.

On a piece of card, draw, colour and cut out a picture of the story's main character. Attach string, wool or ribbon to one corner of the book cover and tape it to the back of your cut-out character. Pop the character into the pocket on the front cover.

You can now let your character 'walk through' the story, or use it as a bookmark.

EXTRA!
Take a close look at *The Jolly Postman* by Janet and Allan Ahlberg.
Think about how you could use envelopes or pockets inside your books.

How to be Brilliant at Making Books

Books on the wall

Any book can be displayed on the wall. It is best to work in pairs or groups so that you can share the work. Negotiate for wall space. You need to know exactly how much space you have so that you can plan how the book will be displayed. Depending on how much space you have you will need to decide whether all your pages will be open or just some of them.

   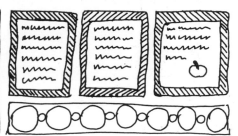

In your group you will need to negotiate to decide who will:

- compose (make up the words)
- edit the book
- design the pages
- write the final copy
- prepare the headings
- draw the illustrations
- put up the display

You might decide to share some of the roles.

Put down all your ideas for your 'book on the wall' here and then share them with the rest of your group.

EXTRA!
Once you have created your book, make three-dimensional shapes and designs to fill in the spaces between pages or sections. Draw lots of attention to your book.

Mini-books

The real fun of making mini-books is that you have to do everything scaled down. Your pages will be tiny so you need to do tiny writing, tiny illustrations, tiny headings and tiny borders.

The most successful mini-books are the ones that are about something really huge, so there's a kind of joke there to start with. For example:

Use this sheet to plan your mini-book:

My mini-book will be:
- concertina
- flick-through
- bound at the top
- bound at the side

My text will be:
- done on the computer
- typed
- handwritten
- joined-up
- in colour
- in black
- stuck on to the pages
- written on the pages

My illustrations will be:
- framed
- not framed
- done with felt tips
- done with crayons
- done with pen
- in bubbles
- cut and pasted
- textured

It will have:
- an unusual shape
- flaps
- windows
- pop-ups

Write an outline for your mini-book here

You might need to use the back of the sheet. You can use this page to design and make several different mini-books.

For my binding I will use:
- sticky tape
- staples
- stitching
- string

EXTRA!
When you have made all the decisions you need to, make your book. Have fun!

How to be Brilliant at Making Books

Who will read it?

All good writers decide who will read their books before they write them. This is because they need to know who the reader is to make sure the book 'fits' them. It wouldn't be any good writing a 'grandad's book' for a little child, or an adventure book for someone who wanted to know how to mend their car.

Choose your reader:
* mum
* dad
* best friend
* young child
* teacher
* other _____

* group of friends
* religious leader
* big brother or sister
* grandparent

Choose a type of book to write:
* story
* how to ... book
* picture story-book
* information book
* dictionary
* collection book
* other _____

This book will suit my reader because:

Its format will be:

My outline:

EXTRA!
When you've worked out everything you need to know, give yourself a check-list and make your book.

Run out of space? Use the back of the sheet.

Scrap-books

Scrap-books can be as interesting and as personal as you like because your audience is *you*!

First, you need to make the scrap-book from sugar paper or card.

You need fairly tough pages because you'll be pasting or gluing quite a lot.

You can choose whatever *you* like to put in *your* scrap-book. Here are some suggestions:
* newspaper/magazine cuttings
* photographs
* certificates
* letters
* favourite things (anything that will stick on to the pages)
* tickets
* programmes
* book reviews

It is important to write captions for each item you stick in. That way when you look through your scrap-book, later, you'll remember why you chose it.

Make a list here of everything you want to include in your scrap-book. Decide what you are going to say in the captions and draft them. Will they be funny? What information will you give?

Use the back of the sheet if you run out of space.

EXTRA!
Get together a collection of things to start your scrap-book. Make a scrap-book about a famous personality or an historical event.

How to be Brilliant at Making Books

Collection books

Make a small collection book with sugar paper or card. Bright colours will give your book added interest.

Decide what you're going to collect.

On each page show:
- the date
- a heading
- a picture of your item
- a description of your item in words

Say why you collected it and where you got it from.

Keep a running total of your collection. If you have different sections, leave plenty of space for things you might want to add later. Give your book a contents page and an index.

List the items you've already got to start a collection with.

Design a collection book for a collector of leaves and flowers.

Continue on the back of the sheet.

EXTRA!
Start a collection. Decide what you could collect easily and cheaply. Maybe your friend would start the same kind of collection and you could compare books.

Albums

An album is a book with blank pages in which you collect things which belong together.

First you need to make your album from sugar paper or card.

Collect all your items together and lay them out flat so that you can look at them and put them into order.

Plan your album here

My album will be for:

I will collect:

I will sort them by:

My captions will tell me:

How will you sort them?

stamps	photos	postcards
by country	by family	by place
by date	by friends	by date
by colour	by date	
by shape		

EXTRA!
Collect any old family photos and postcards you can, and begin your album. Share it with a friend.

How to be Brilliant at Making Books

Diaries and journals

Diaries and journals are very similar types of books. In both you write down a regular record of what is happening. Diaries tend to be more private than journals.

You can start a diary or journal at any time. All you need are some pages bound together to make a book. Work out your format first. Decide how often you will write and how long you will keep your diary or journal for. Divide the book into sections. Use a calendar to help you get the days and dates right.

If you are making a diary you could start by writing family and friends' birthdays in the right sections.

You can write your entries straight into your book or you can write them on sheets of paper, and cut and stick. Careful design of the pages and illustrations will make your book more interesting. You could add snippets from the newspaper that are of particular interest to you.

Design and write/illustrate your first entry here, to cut and stick.

EXTRA!
You could make a personal organizer by using a small ring binder.
You will need to make diary pages, a calendar, notebook pages, address and phone number pages. What else might you find useful?

Making a group book

The good thing about working in a group or team to make a book is that you can combine everybody's good ideas together.

History, science, geography and RE topics make good group book projects.

There are two types of group book.

Type A
With this type, each person does part of the writing and illustrating and has their own work included.

Type B
In the other type, members of the team are given different roles or jobs such as editor or illustrator and do only those (for everybody's work).

Get your team together. Decide how you will work.

Who	What	How	Why	When	Where
Katie	edits	on the computer	because she's fastest	when the writers have finished	classroom

Make a list on the back of the sheet of all the things you will need to gather together before you begin.

> **EXTRA!**
> When you have worked on one kind of group book, try working on the other (Type A or B).
> Which works best for you? Which method gives your team the best results?

Class books

Class books can be about anything and everything. Discuss your theme or topic first, so that everybody knows what's expected.

Choose someone to put the book together, using sugar paper or card.

Make your own piece of work the very best you can do, in content and presentation.

When everybody's piece of work is stuck in, go through and fill any spaces with jokes, patterns, illustrations and messages.

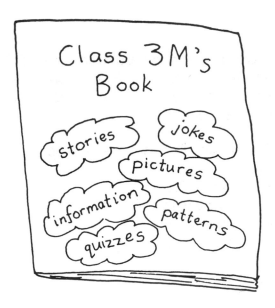

Draft a piece for your class book here, on the theme of sports and games. Try to make yours different from everybody else's.

EXTRA!
Write out some jokes, and draw some coloured patterns to fill in the gaps.

Swap-with-a-friend books

Work with a friend. Each make a book. Try to make your books 'twins' of each other. Help each other with the design of the books and with ideas for things to include. Give your books extra special titles.

Decide on rules for book-swapping. Will you swap:
- every day
- every week
- once a fortnight
- at weekends only

You decide!

You can use any paper you like, so long as you can write and draw on it

Write whatever you want in your book, then pass it to your friend who will read what you've written and respond to it by writing back to you.

Here are some of the things you can write for each other:
- messages
- poems
- stories
- secrets

- letters
- ideas
- games
- can you think of any other ideas?

Use this page to design your books and write your first messages to each other. Remember, when you get your friend's book you must respond to her writing too.

EXTRA!
Ask your teacher if you can have a special book-swapping time every week.

Poetry anthologies

A collection of poems in a book is called an anthology.
In your anthology you could have:

- your own poems
- copies of poems that you specially like
- friends' favourite poems
- poems to read aloud
- poems to share

You can have an anthology made entirely by you, or with a friend, a group anthology, or a class anthology.

Plan what your anthology will look like here:

How will you keep your poems clean and tidy while you're putting your anthology together?

Type of book	**Where will you get the poems?**	**What will the pages look like?**
• concertina	• write them	• decorated
• mini	• copy them out	• illustrated
• shape		

Plan your contents page here:

_____ by _____

_____ by _____

_____ by _____

_____ by _____

_____ by _____

_____ by _____

EXTRA!
Write some poems to go into a friend's anthology.

Picture story-books

First of all, decide who you're making your picture story-book for. Think about the things that would interest your reader. Aim for a small number of pages for your first book. Eight is plenty.

Work out an outline of the story in notes. Plan exactly what illustrations and words will be on each page by drawing matchstick people sketches in these boxes.

Title page

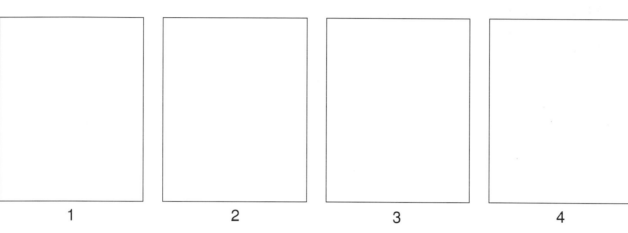

1   2   3   4

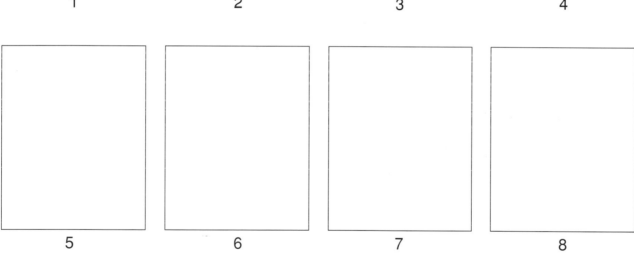

5   6   7   8

When you've planned everything, begin to write and draw your story using separate pieces of paper. This saves the problem of what you do if you make mistakes. When all the pages are done, cut and paste.

EXTRA!
Test the book out on your chosen reader and others.

How to be Brilliant at Making Books

Talking books

Everybody enjoys listening to a good story. You will need a tape recorder with a microphone and a cassette tape.

Decide who will listen to your story and what it will be about.

Write your story here. Make it dramatic. Get lots of description into it so that the listener can imagine the scenes happening.

Read your story aloud to a friend to get their ideas and comments. Re-draft your story.

Practise getting the words and your tone of voice just right. Then record your story. You could ask a friend to do sound effects.

EXTRA!
Find out about Talking Books and Talking Newspapers. Who do you think uses them?
Where might you find out more about them?

Books for information

There are all kinds of books that give you information:

- books about topics
- atlases (books of maps)
- books of recipes
- encyclopaediae
- dictionaries

How many more can you think of?

To make your own information book, first make a list of topics you might write about. Decide which one you will begin with.

Next, choose how you want to organize your book. Will it be in chapters or organized alphabetically like an encyclopaedia?

Your next task is information-gathering, but before you do that you need to know exactly what information you will need and where you will find it. Brainstorm here:

My topic is:

What I need to know   **Where I will get the information**

EXTRA!
While you're gathering information, keep it safe in a folder. Then put it all
into order before you start to write your book.

How to be Brilliant at Making Books

Books of retold stories

Choose a favourite story or novel to retell.

List some of your favourites here, then choose.

_____   _____

_____   _____

_____   _____

_____   _____

_____

Divide the story into small sections or chapters, so that you have one section or chapter on each page.

You will need to know the story very well. It's a good idea to reread parts of it as you're writing to make sure you don't miss important points out. Use the story as a model for your own book.

Your title should be the same as the real one, but instead of giving an author you write 'Retold by....'

Write your text and do your illustrations on spare paper. When you have finished, stick them into the book. (This saves you having to worry about mistakes.)

Design your page layouts and plan your illustrations here.

EXTRA!
Write a review of the retold book for the back cover. Better still, get a friend to read your book and write the review instead.

You might need to use the back of the sheet.

Make an official family history book

You can use any format you like to make your official family history book; the important thing is to get hold of as much information as you can. You will need to interview as many members of the family as possible. Get them to give you their family memories to write into your book.

First of all, make a list of the people who might help you with your research:

great grandparents
grandparents
parents
aunts and uncles
cousins
brothers and sisters

Divide your book into sections. It can include things like:

Begin here by writing some of your own best family memories. They may be good, bad, happy, sad, funny, jokey – anything you like.

Run out of space? Use the back of the sheet!

EXTRA!
Make a section of family portraits. Draw them yourself rather than use photographs.
(But you can use photographs too if you like!) Some members of the
family might let you copy their birth or wedding certificates into the books.
They'll certainly all love reading it when it's finished.

How to be Brilliant at Making Books

How to ... books

Books that tell you how to do something are excellent for learning new skills and ideas.

You have to write very clearly and carefully so that the reader can understand and follow the instructions. The instructions must be in the right order.

You also need to be able to draw very careful diagrams.

Practise one of these here:

How to make your favourite sandwich

or

How to make a cup of tea

You could do a How to... book for a sport or game, for example:
*   football
*   rounders
*   hopscotch

EXTRA!
Make a list of skills and interests for which you could write How to... books.
Choose one and make the book.

How to be Brilliant at Making Books

Check-list of things to think about when making books

What kind of book have you chosen to do?

How will you get started?

What will you need?

Where will you get those things?

How much time will you need?

Will you work with someone else? If so, who will do what?

What help might you need?

Will you be able to use the computer? For which parts?

Have you decided on lettering styles and page layouts?

How many pages will your book have?

How will you bind your book?

How will you illustrate your book?

What's your deadline or publication date?

Use this check-list whenever you make a book

Glossary

alliteration
When words begin with the same initial sound or letter.

binding
The way the pages of the book are held together.

chapters
The sections a book may be divided into.

content
Everything that goes into the book.

copyright
The right to publish. Symbolized by ©.

deadline
The date your work must be ready by.

format
The shape and style of the book.

headings
These are the titles given to chapters or sections in your book.

illustration
Sometimes called 'artwork'. The pictures in the book.

index
Alphabetical list, showing you which pages will tell you about subjects in the book.

ISBN
International Standard Book Number – every published book has a number through which it can be tracked down.

lettering styles
Different ways of printing; in type they are called 'fonts'.

outline
A rough draft of the essential parts of the text or story only.

page layout
The design of each page.

presentation
How your book/writing/pages look.

Publishing jobs

author
The person who writes the book and gives it to the publisher for publication.

editor
The person who prepares the book for publication.

graphic designer
The person who works out the layout of the book and designs its pages.

illustrator
The person who draws the pictures.

printer
The person or company who makes multiple copies of the book for the publisher.

publisher
The person or company who makes the decision whether to publish the book and looks after the costs of the project.